POSTERS

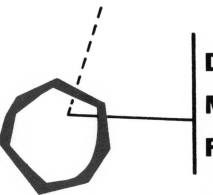

DESIGNING
MAKING
REPRODUCING

George F. Horn

ART TEACHER AND SUPERVISOR,
Baltimore, Maryland Public Schools

DAVIS PUBLICATIONS, INC. **Worcester, Massachusetts**

Distributed by
STERLING PUBLISHING CO., INC.
419 Park Avenue South
New York, N. Y. 10016

Library of Congress
Catalog Card
No. 64-12774
SBN 87192-020-4

▼

Copyright 1964

Davis Publications, I

Worcester
Massachusetts
Fifth Printing 1972

Poster, courtesy Pan American Airlines

CONTENTS

PREFACE

The designing and making of posters is one of the most popular forms of art expression in the public schools.

It is a regular part of the art program in developing the student's understanding of lettering, illustration, and layout as they relate to commercial art.

In addition, the poster has found its way into many aspects of school life outside of the art room—promoting safety, health, school plays, athletic events, and other like activities.

The role of the poster even extends into the community where students make designs for a variety of city-wide projects, such as clean-up campaigns, crime prevention, brotherhood, and pedestrian safety programs.

This book, with its analysis of the poster, its many practical suggestions for making posters, plus the outstanding examples of student and professional posters, has been prepared as an aid to students who will be participating in this exciting form of visual expression.

It is hoped that the effort behind the organization and preparation of the material in this book will result in raising the quality of student poster design.

The author wishes to express his appreciation for the sincere cooperation of the following for their contribution of outstanding poster examples used throughout the book:

WITHDRAWN

MR. WALTER M. HENSHEL
Braniff International Airways
Dallas, Texas

ITALIAN STATE TOURIST OFFICE
Palazzo D'Italia—Rockefeller Center
New York, New York

MR. IRVIN S. TAUBKIN
New York Times

DR. GEORGE E. MOORE
Roswell Park Memorial Institute
Buffalo, New York

DR. ROBERT D. GOLDMAN
Assistant Director of Art Education
Philadelphia Public Schools
Philadelphia, Pennsylvania

RUTH B. KOONS
Philadelphia Savings Fund Society

MR. BRADLEY L. COLEY, JR.
Pepsi-Cola Company

YOULDON C. HOWELL
Coordinator
Pasadena City Schools
Pasadena, California

MISS NANCY CARTER
National Dairy Council

MR. WILLIAM PRINCE
Instructor
Maryland Art Institute
Baltimore, Maryland

MR. NORMAN WHITE
Art Director
Donnelly Outdoor Advertising
Baltimore, Maryland

MR. R. JAMES WELLS
Chase Manhattan Bank
New York, New York

MR. LEW WAGGAMAN
Art Director
Van Sant, Dugdale
Baltimore, Maryland

ADLER-SCHWARTZ ART STUDIO
Baltimore, Maryland

MR. AL HURWITZ
Supervisor of Art
Dade County Schools
Miami, Florida

MR. SAUL SCHUR
Seventeen Magazine
New York, New York

HELEN M. STAHL
Art Teacher
Treadwell School
Memphis, Tennessee

MR. J. P. REARDON
Art Teacher
Classical High School
Worcester, Massachusetts

THE MUSEUM OF CONTEMPORARY
CRAFTS
New York, New York

DR. LEVIN C. LEATHERBURY
Supervisor of Art
San Diego City Schools
San Diego, California

MR. NELSON ADLIN
Art Teacher
Eastern High School
Baltimore, Maryland

MR. MARVIN VON SCHULZ
Art Teacher
Mergenthaler-Vocational Technical
   High School
Baltimore, Maryland

DELTA AIRLINES
Atlanta, Georgia

AMERICAN AIRLINES
New York, New York

OLIVE JOBES
Supervisor of Art
Baltimore County Public Schools
Maryland

ELIZABETH H. GILLIGAN
Director of Fine Arts
Boston Public Schools
Boston, Massachusetts

RICHARD HOWARD
Art Chairman
Nathan Hale High School
Tulsa, Oklahoma

MR. RICHARD L. MICHERDZINSKI
Director of Art
Baltimore City Public Schools
Baltimore, Maryland

PAN AMERICAN AIRLINES
New York, New York

MR. HENRI GHENT
Assistant Director
Brooklyn Institute of Arts and Sciences
Brooklyn, New York

MRS. EVELYN FARLAND
Poster Originals, Limited
New York

MR. PAUL HARRIS
Coordinator of Educational Services
Museum of Modern Art
New York

MRS. VERA LIST
List Art Posters
Boston and New York City

Posters take many and varied forms. Some are tall and narrow, others, low and long. There are multi-colored posters as well as some quite effective designs limited to one or two colors. Posters may be three-dimensional as well as two-dimensional.

Posters appear in stores and store windows; at the entrance of places of amusement and entertainment; on buses and streetcars in the form of car cards; in subways; on the back of taxis and the sides of trucks; along the highways as billboards. Posters are a very colorful part of travel bureaus; airline, railway and bus terminals. They may be seen announcing the latest in movies, plays, and aspirin, on the approaches to a big city; selling feed and seed, on the side of a barn in the country.

The poster tersely calls upon the reader to buy, try, drink, think, visit, travel, see, walk, run, drive, fly, cruise, taste, feel, smell. This universally-used medium of the graphic arts industry is ever-present, hawking the wares and services of manufacturers and businesses.

The poster is also a very popular art form in the schools. Not only is it an interesting activity in the art program, but it also plays a vital role in the promoting of the school program. There are posters on health, school rules, plays, dances, athletic events, holidays, seasons of the year, clubs, organizations, community events, and various phases of the school curriculum.

With this brief summary of the many-faceted role of the poster, let us consider those things which are necessary in the designing of an effective poster.

ROLE
OF THE POSTER

THE MUSEUM OF CONTEMPORARY CRAFTS N.Y.

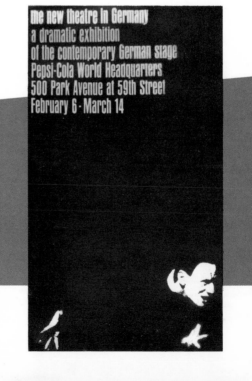

the new theatre in Germany
a dramatic exhibition
of the contemporary German stage
Pepsi-Cola World Headquarters
500 Park Avenue at 59th Street
February 6 - March 14

The basic difference between the poster and other advertising media is that the poster speaks to an audience "on the move." Newspaper ads, magazine ads, and mailing pieces such as folders, brochures and booklets, are designed for the reader who has some time to stand or sit and read for a while. This material can, and usually does, include more detailed information, and if it is attractively designed, will be read.

On the other hand, the poster must capture the attention of its audience and get the message across in a matter of seconds. It must spark the reader to take the desired action through a brief message packed with punch or veiled in subtlety. If it does not do this, it has failed in its mission.

While there are literally hundreds of uses for the poster, it will have only one of four possible purposes:

1. TO ANNOUNCE AN EVENT

(Continued)

Diary Of
ANNE
FRANK

2.   TO PROMOTE A SERVICE

3.   TO SELL A PRODUCT

CHARACTERISTICS
OF THE POSTER

The single fact that the poster is designed for an audience that is moving distinguishes it from all other promotional media. However, there are certain characteristics in addition to this that should be considered. Some of these may not be limited to the poster alone, but all should serve as guiding factors in the designing of a poster:

1. A successful poster tells the story quickly, boldly, in a direct way. Extraneous matter should be dropped at the outset of the design. It should be brief, clear, pointed. There should be as few elements as possible included in the design. Only information that is absolutely necessary to tell the story should become a part of the poster.

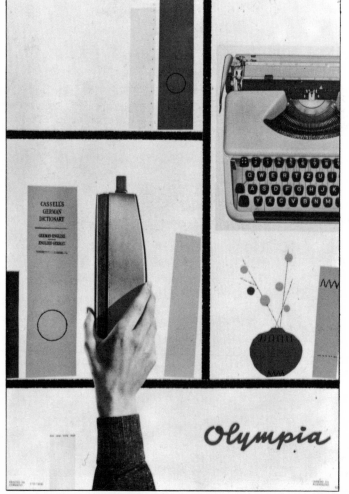

2. It must be attention-getting. If the poster goes unnoticed, it isn't worth the paper on which it is printed.

3. The poster must be convincing.

4. A striking use of color is important. This does not necessarily mean an unlimited range of colors. Many times an idea can be presented with greater impact by using one or two colors.

5. An effective poster reflects an almost stark simplicity. Complex arrangement of copy and intricate design only serve to confuse.

Exhibition-Fair
of Contemporary
Art

Florence

23rd March

Aim for an unusual treatment of the elements to be incorporated into the design. Uniqueness in any design problem is a most favorable characteristic. In the poster it is even more necessary. Strive for that which is different in planning to communicate an idea through the poster.

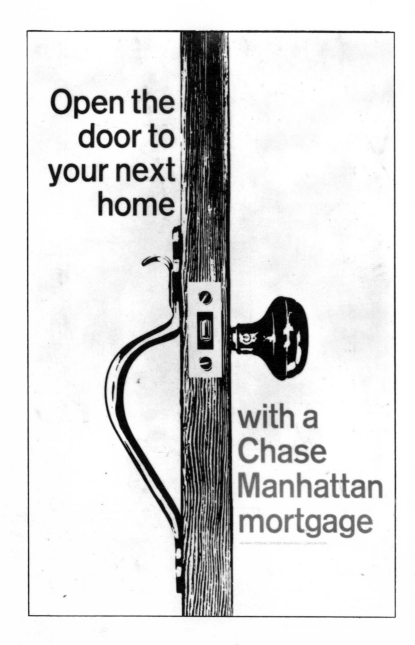

A design is well organized and successful when it reflects certain basic qualities. These design qualities will be discussed briefly as they relate specifically to the poster. They should be considered in the designing of a poster as well as in the evaluation of the finished product.

1. A basic quality, characteristic of all acceptable design, is BALANCE. All of the component parts of the poster should be brought into a carefully related arrangement so delicately balanced that to move one part would unbalance the entire arrangement. There are two kinds of balance:

(Continued)

A. FORMAL BALANCE

Formal balance is also referred to as symmetrical design. If a poster, based on formal balance, were divided down the middle, one side would be exactly the same as the other, as a rule. A design based on strict, formal balance is often thought of as being restful, conservative, serene, and lacking the attention-getting characteristics of an informal design. On the other hand, some very strikingly-dramatic and imaginative posters have been based on formal balance. A generous use of white space, simplicity in illustration, sharp contrasting colors, and a wise selection of letter style are contributing factors to the success of a formally-balanced poster.

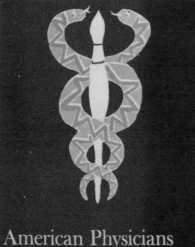

American Physicians
Art Association
an exhibition at
Pepsi-Cola World Headquarters
500 Park Avenue, New York
June 27 to July 7.

Save for a sunny stay
Open a Chase Manhattan
savings account

Brazil: new imag
an exhibition of sculpture & photography at the P
Exhibition Gallery 500 Park Ave., March 27 throug

FROM AN ORIGINAL POSTER DESIGNED BY ARLENE SHANDER, OVERBROOK HIGH SCHOOL. SCHOLARSHIP AWARD 1961 THRIFT POSTER EXHIBIT.

B. INFORMAL BALANCE

A poster based on informal balance presents a design with variations on either side of an imaginary central vertical axis. A large element placed near the center on one side may be balanced by a smaller element positioned farther from the center on the other side. Informal balance provides greater flexibility with more opportunity for unusual arrangement. A well thought out informal design is active, attention-getting and reflects a certain spontaneity.

19

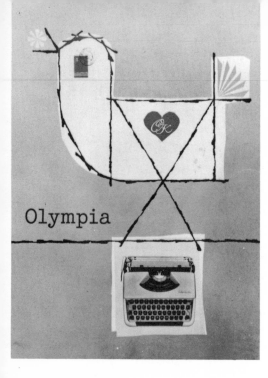

Olympia

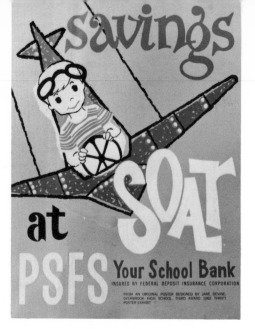

2. Another quality, MOVEMENT, is the systematic directing of the viewer's eye from one part of the poster to another in a way predetermined by the artist. The poster should be designed so that the various points are made in order of importance. Movement may be achieved in a poster through:

A. LINES, AN ARROW

(Continued)

B. BACKGROUND SHAPES AND PANELS

C. GROUPING OF THE ELEMENTS

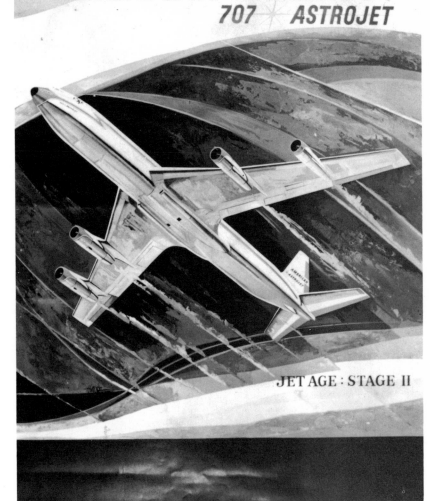

AMERICAN AIRLINES
707 ASTROJET

JET AGE : STAGE II

D. AN ACTION ILLUSTRATION

3. A poster is designed around two or three or more component parts. If each of these were treated with the same importance, the results would be somewhat flat. Therefore, EMPHASIS is a vital concern in the developing of the poster design. Emphasis may be attained by making one part (slogan, illustration) of the design large, then subordinating each of the other parts to this in order of importance. The quality of emphasis may also be achieved by using:

A. **CONTRASTING BACKGROUND SHAPES BEHIND THE ILLUSTRATION OR LETTERING.**

B. **STRONGLY-CONTRASTING COLORS AND VALUES.**

C. A GENEROUS USE OF WHITE SPACE OR OPEN
    SPACE.

★ The American Flag: An Exhibition
at the Pepsi-Cola World Headquarters
500 Park Avenue, July 2nd to July 27th

D. CONTRASTING STYLES, SIZES AND COLORS IN
    LETTERING.

. A LARGE ILLUSTRATION.

4. The poster should be designed so that no one part should dominate in such a way that it becomes greater than the total design. The component parts of the poster also should be arranged so that they "hold together." This is the quality of design referred to as UNITY. All of the parts of the poster should be designed to appear as a single unit. Unity may be attained:

A. THROUGH OVERLAPPING OF THE ELEMENTS IN THE DESIGN.

RIGGS - WARFIELD - ROLOSON

B. THROUGH THE USE OF PANELS, OR A LINE.

C. BY THE TREATMENT OF THE BACKGROUND.

AMERICAN SHIPS EXPAND TRADE AND TRAVEL

5. Another design quality that contributes to an effective poster is SPECIFIC APPEAL. A poster is designed for a specific purpose based on a single theme. Aim to put into the design a "feeling" for the product, service, event, or attitude:

A. A POSTER ADVERTISING PERFUME MAY BE LIGHT, DELICATE, FEMININE, DECORATIVE.

B. A POSTER SELLING TRUCKS OR HEAVY INDUSTRIAL EQUIPMENT SHOULD BE STRONG, HEAVY, MASCULINE, WITH BOLD COLORS.

C. A POSTER ENCOURAGING A WINTER VACATION IN THE SOUTH SHOULD BE LIGHT, SUNSHINY, GAY, CAREFREE.

TOYS FROM ALL OVER

An Exhibition at Pepsi-Cola World Headquarters, 500 Park Ave. from January 30th through March 14th. Free European puppet shows daily.

Apply these design qualities to your poster design. Aim for simplicity and legibility. Strive for the unusual to get and hold attention.

COLOR
IN THE POSTER

A knowledge of the nature and characteristics of color as well as how it should be used is prerequisite to successful poster design.

One of the simplest ways to acquire a "feeling" for color is by examining the many different kinds of commercially-printed materials that are available—posters, billboards, car cards, folders, booklets, magazine ads, packages. Study the way in which color is distributed throughout the design; how colors relate to each other; different degrees of contrast in various color combinations; the way color is used to reflect the theme of the design. Since color plays such an important part in poster design, a study as suggested here will be of immeasurable help in planning and completing a poster.

There are many standard color schemes, formulae, and theories that have been developed to aid the artist in his use of color. A study of these certainly would contribute to a broader knowledge of the characteristics of color. However, a practical understanding of color can be acquired best by actually working with color. Mix different colors together in varying proportions and note what happens. Try using white paint in colors. Experiment with black and see how it affects the different colors.

COLOR ATTRACTS

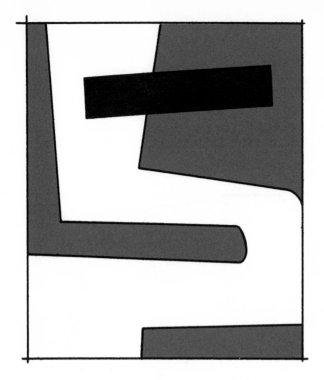

COLOR MAY BE USED SIMPLY
BECAUSE IT LOOKS GOOD

COLOR IDENTIFIES

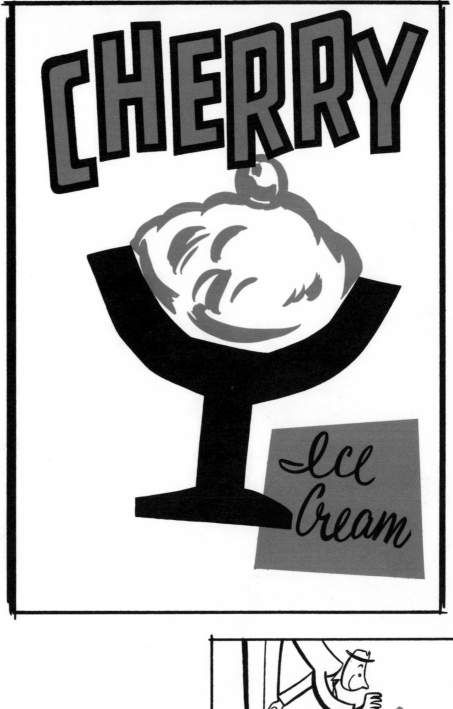

COLOR MAY EXPRESS A FEELING FOR
THE IDEA BEING PRESENTED

WHEN USED THROUGHOUT THE POSTER,
COLOR CREATES MOVEMENT, UNITY

A COLOR BACKGROUND DEVELOPS
ORDERLINESS, CONTINUITY, CONTRAST

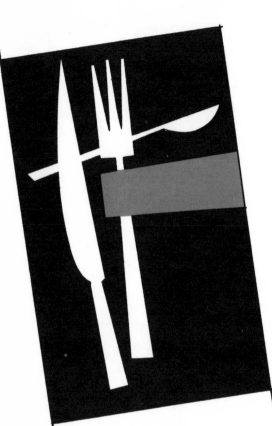

Colors and values used in combinations affect each other. A dark object on a light background will appear smaller than the same object, light on a dark background. Combinations of colors that are closely related, such as orange and red, produce subtle relationships. Whereas, colors with strong differences in value as well as color combinations that are opposite in nature (orange and blue, green and red) will give sharper contrasts.

Explore the potential of color. Experiment with many different combinations—light with dark, bright with dull. Think in terms of specific uses for color. A working knowledge of the possibilities of color is essential to good poster design.

Lettering for posters should be simple, legible, appropriate, and attractive. There is no place in poster design for lettering that is overly-tricky, confusing and difficult to read. The success of the poster depends as much on the selection of letter style as on any other phase of the design.

There are a number of good lettering books available which may be used to develop an understanding of the characteristics of different styles of letters. A study of current advertising material is valuable in acquiring an understanding of the ways in which lettering can be used effectively. Note in this material the style, size and color of the lettering as it relates to the rest of the design and to the purpose of the ad or poster.

39

Hand lettering has a great deal of flexibility. Letters may be bold or light; straight or italic; condensed, normal, extended. There may be combinations of capitals with lower-case letters, capitals and small capitals, or the use of all capitals or all lower case. However, once it has been decided which direction the lettering should take, it should be carried out with consistency. If a word is started with a condensed letter, the entire word should be done in this manner.

BOLD LIGHT

STRAIGHT
ITALIC

CONDENSED
NORMAL
EXTENDED

American Ships
Expand
Trade and Travel

BREAKFAST
might have helped!

1964

VINTER OLYMPICS
INNSBRUCK
AUSTRIA

TANGLEWOOD
lenox, mass.
aug. 23

An ability to letter can be developed only through frequent study and practice. In lettering, observe the following:

Safety

1. GUIDE LINES

Guide lines are used so the letters in a word or series of words will be uniform in size as well as be kept on a predetermined line. The size of the letter desired will determine the space between guide lines. For capital letters two guide lines are necessary, one for the top of the letter and the other for the bottom. There may be a need for four guide lines when lettering lower-case letters— two for the center body, one for the ascenders and one for the descenders. It is also helpful to use vertical guide lines to keep the letters uniformly straight. Slanted guide lines will assure a consistent angle in italic letters.

2. SPACING

The amount of space between letters in a word should be equal. Due to the irregular shape of some letters, they cannot be spaced mechanically. Good lettering is achieved through optical spacing. In lettering a word, the artist moves some letters closer and some farther apart to get an equal amount of space between each letter in the word. Usually more space is automatically left between straight-edge letters.

3. UNIFORMITY

There should be a uniformity of weight of the letters within a word. In using Gothic letters, for example, all of the letters in a word should be the same thickness. With Roman letters, all the thin strokes should be the same weight as well as all of the thick strokes.

Lettering for posters may be done in a number of ways using an assortment of tools and materials. A widely-used technique is to block in or draw in the letters first and then paint them. After determining the words to be lettered, style to be used, space in which words are to appear, size of lettering, proceed to sketch in words to fit space. Working over this, draw in or block in each letter accurately and then fill them in with paint. For sharper letters, a ruling pen may be used on the edges before painting them in.

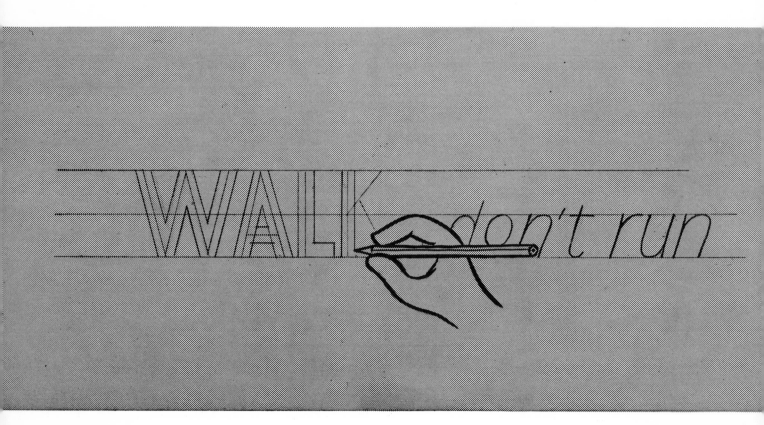

Another technique is to letter directly with a lettering brush. This is often referred to as single-stroke lettering. First, draw the guide lines and space the letters in the desired position, then paint the letters. The thickness of the letters will be determined by the size of the lettering brush. There are also a variety of lettering tools, including the felt-tip pen, available to the poster artist; they come in different sizes and shapes, according to the size and style of letters desired. To become proficient in the use of the lettering brush and lettering pens, practice vertical, horizontal and curved strokes first, then practice lettering words using simple styles of letters.

Letters cut from colored paper can be very effective for use on a poster. Cut-paper letters also give you a certain amount of flexibility that you cannot otherwise get. Once the letters are cut out they may be tried in a number of different ways on the poster before they are pasted down. To assure uniformity of size of letters, first cut a strip of paper to the size the letters should be. Fold this paper in equal parts, according to the desired width of the letters. Then, cut one letter from each fold. The "M" and "W" being wide letters would require the space of approximately 1½ folds. The "I", of course, would be less than one fold.

While it is true that simplicity should be the guide for poster lettering, it cannot be overlooked that some themes and slogans suggest an illustrated type of lettering. Used in a limited way, expressive lettering can be effective.

In a slogan of several words there may be one word you wish to emphasize over the others.   There are a number of ways you may do this:

1. By making the one word larger
2. By changing the value or color of this word
3. By changing the style of lettering for this word
4. By lettering the word in capitals while using lower-case letters for the rest of the slogan
5. By underlining the one word
6. By lettering this word in Italic letters

WALK --DON'T RUN!

WALK-DON'T RUN!

WALK -- *don't Run!*

WALK-don't run!

WALK-DON'T RUN!

WALK-DON'T RUN

DRINK MILK
for HEALTH
CGJSWXYZ
abegjkmt 24
3568 MILK

SUPPORT YOUR TEAM

CBJKVWXabce
fghjkmvz 1234

practice
OFTEN

GAME TODAY! BHJKN SWXZ

study ab letter jkv form

Save Money Toda
ABEGHKDJQ
bfghiklrsz 456

PRACTICE
makes makes
PERFECT
Results

Join a CLUB!
DEKMRSTX
WZ bcefkrtv
TRY
OTHER
STYLES

drafting machine...

CHRISTMAS

One Dozen

Find out about the

MEDFORD'S

CHOCOLATE BARK

Swan

DESIGNING THE POSTER

Before actually designing the poster you must familiarize yourself with the topic for a particular poster. Gather all of the pertinent facts. Know as much as you can about your topic.

Start organizing this information in terms of:

    A. A SLOGAN

    B. AN ILLUSTRATION

    C. A TRADEMARK

    D. THE NAME OF THE PRODUCT, SERVICE OR EVENT

    E. TIME, PLACE AND DATE

    F. PRICE

In most cases, the poster would not include all of these— only that which is important to getting the complete message across. A brief slogan, a striking illustration and a minimum of additional reading matter should be the aim.

Determine the size and shape of the poster; the emphasis; the number of colors to be used. Is it to be a "one shot" design or will it be reproduced? If it is to be reproduced, you should know by what process. (Certain methods for reproducing posters in quantity are discussed in another chapter of this book.) These are technicalities that must be considered in the pre-design stage of poster making.

With this background, you should now be ready to design the poster. A suggested procedure follows:

1. Develop small preliminary sketches, often referred to as "thumbnail" sketches. They must be in proportion to the finished, full-size poster. The purpose of these sketches is:

   A. TO TRY DIFFERENT WAYS OF ARRANGING THE INFORMATION ON THE POSTER, TO EXPLORE MANY DESIGN POSSIBILITIES.

   B. TO TRY DIFFERENT STYLES AND SIZES OF LETTERS.

   C. TO DEVELOP VARIOUS COLOR COMBINATIONS.

   D. TO EXPERIMENT WITH BACKGROUND SHAPES, PANELS, LINES OF MOVEMENT.

   E. TO TRY DIFFERENT EMPHASES.

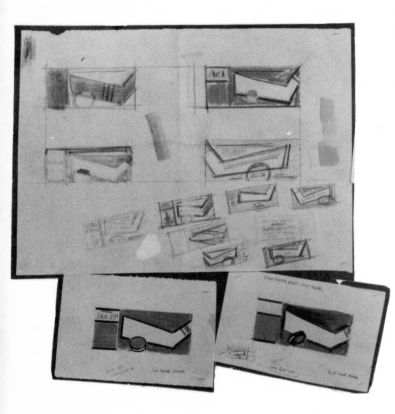

The preliminary sketch is the most important part of the poster, for out of it comes the final design. This is where you crystallize your thinking and visualize an idea. It is at this stage of poster design that you make direct application of the design qualities desired in a poster as well as the suggestions on color discussed earlier in this book. In the preliminary sketch you determine the style of lettering, the distribution of colors, the type of illustration, the layout of the poster. These sketches should be carefully developed to the point that they look like miniature posters.

Keep in mind that, above everything else, a poster must be easy to read. A common error in poster design is a disjointed arrangement of the wording in the slogan. When the slogan is broken up, the thought behind it can get lost. The slogan should appear as it would normally be read. If the poster includes other information, such as a time, date, and place, it should be treated as a unit and not spread out in different sections of the poster.

Another common error is the excessive angling of words in an attempt to achieve the unusual. This usually obscures the message and should be avoided.

Vertical lettering is rarely successful and also should be avoided.

2. From your preliminary sketches, select the one that you feel has the best possibilities. Working with a pencil on tracing paper, enlarge this sketch to the full size of the poster. There are several techniques for scaling a small, preliminary sketch up to the final size of the poster.

A. Be sure your sketch is in proportion to the full size of the poster. For example, if the finished poster is to be 22″ x 28″, the sketch may be $\frac{1}{4}$ size, or 5$\frac{1}{2}$″ x 7″. Then simply multiply everything on the sketch by four to complete the enlarged drawing.

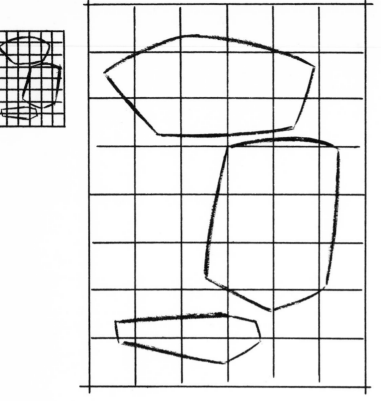

B. Or, for the same size poster, you may block the sketch off in ¼″ blocks, the tracing paper in 1″ blocks, and proceed with the enlargement of your sketch, following the blocks.

C. Another technique is to draw lines on the sketch and the tracing paper, diagonally from corner to corner, vertically up the middle and horizontally across the center. As you enlarge the sketch you check it against these lines.

D. The sketch may also be "blown" up by using a balloptican or a pantograph.

All of the drawing, erasing, re-drawing and final-izing of the poster design is done on this tracing. It should be complete as well as accurate in every detail.

3. Trace this master drawing onto the poster board and complete the poster. Refer to the preliminary sketch for the colors to be used.

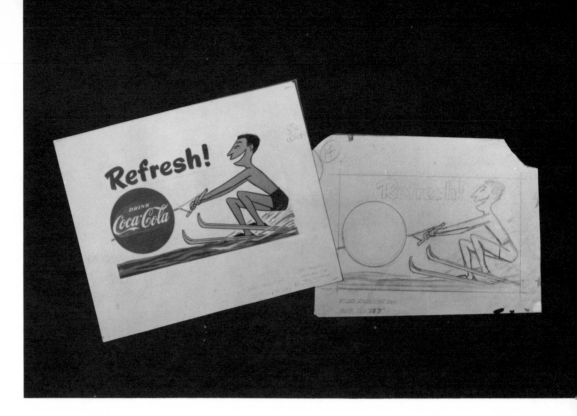

Develop good work habits and high standards of craftsmanship as you complete the poster.

1. Be sure that your hands are clean and free of paint so that you don't get fingerprints on the poster.

2. Keep the brushes clean. If paint gets on the ferrule or handle, wash it off.

3. Have plenty of clean water available for mixing colors and rinsing brushes.

4. Be sure you have plenty of space for the materials you will be using.

5. Be sure the paint is the right consistency. A good technique for assuring this is to use a scrap of poster board as an intermediate step between the jar of paint and the poster. Put some paint from the jar on this piece of poster board and brush it out, adding water as necessary. When it is just right, apply it to the poster. Never work directly from the jar of paint to the poster.

6. Work for steady, sharp edges, particularly in lettering. Ragged lettering is unattractive and ineffective.

SUGGESTIONS FOR VARIETY IN DESIGN

While the procedure discussed earlier in this chapter for designing a poster emphasizes the two-dimensional poster and the use of poster paints, there are other interesting techniques that may be employed to get greater variety.

A. DESIGNING WITH COLORED PAPER

Using colored paper cut a shape to represent the illustration, making it the size it is to be on the completed poster. Then cut strips of colored paper to represent the slogan. Place these elements on a piece of poster board of the desired size and color. Move them around, trying different arrangements. After determining the right design, complete the illustration and cut the letters for the slogan from the strips of colored paper. Place these parts back on the poster board in the position previously decided upon for a final evaluation. Make whatever changes that are necessary and paste the illustration and slogan in postion.

This technique for designing a poster offers a great deal of flexibility since the design is never really final until all of its parts are pasted down.

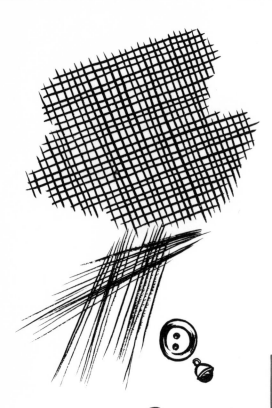

B. DESIGNING WITH A VARIETY OF MATERIALS

An elaboration on designing with colored paper is the introduction of other materials that lend themselves to poster design. Cloth, burlap, straw, buttons, metallic paper, cardboard, textured papers and boards, wool and many other interesting items may be brought into poster design. Basic to successful use of these materials is the preliminary planning recommended earlier in this chapter. One caution would be to limit the number of different materials. When too much variety exists in this respect the poster can lose its effect.

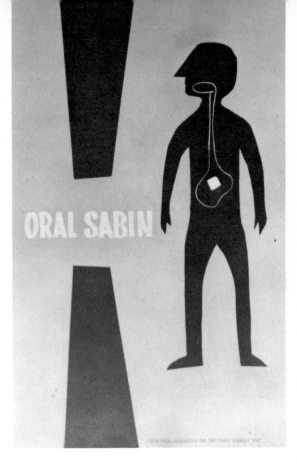

C. THREE-DIMENSIONAL POSTERS

3-D techniques may be used in a limited way as a point of emphasis or generally throughout the entire poster. Some of the most effective uses of 3-D in a poster have been in building up part of the illustration or a key word in a slogan.

The 3-D poster is designed in much the same way as any other kind of poster—preliminary sketches, color sketch, master drawing. However, in its final rendering it differs in that certain procedures for getting 3-D effects are brought into play. Following are a few suggestions for getting 3-D effects in a poster:

1. LETTERING

Three-dimensional effects may be achieved by cutting letters out of poster board and setting them out from the background by gluing small blocks of wood between the letters and the background.

The slogan may also be lettered on a panel of poster board, this panel then being attached to the poster to give a 3-D effect.

If a cutawl is available, 3-D letters may be cut from thick material (wall board) and glued on the poster for a 3-D effect.

2. ILLUSTRATION

Through the use of paper sculpture techniques, striking 3-D illustrations can be made out of colored paper and attached in position on the poster.

3-D illustrations may also be made by building up on the poster board with papier-mâché.

Another 3-D technique is to cut out a flat illustration and set it out from the background on small wood blocks.

These are just some of the ways by which there can be a broader interpretation of design in a poster. Think creatively and aim for uniqueness in design.

REFERENCE FILE

An excellent way to cultivate a "feeling" for good poster design is to study those outstanding posters that surround us in our everyday life. Along with this would be the development of a reference file to include varied examples of illustrations, design and lettering that will be of assistance in the designing of posters. Business and industry spend millions of dollars each year in the preparation of attractive printed matter for public consumption. There is a wealth of this material at hand which may be easily obtained and organized into a reference file. Layout techniques, color combinations, illustrations, and lettering styles in magazine ads, folders, brochures, booklets, packages, often relate very closely to poster treatment and can be helpful in broadening the thinking of the poster designer. Start developing a reference file now in order to become better acquainted with advertising layout techniques in general.

REPRODUCTION TECHNIQUES APPROPRIATE FOR SCHOOL POSTERS

A single poster design may be reproduced many times by one of several available printing processes. When a poster is to be reproduced in vast quantities commercially, it is often done by the letterpress printing process or by planographic printing, also known as offset lithography. Since it is unlikely that either of these two methods would be used for most school purposes it is sufficient to merely mention them here. It is recommended, however, that a visit to a letterpress and an offset printing plant would be desirable to acquire an understanding of the steps involved in each printing process. Such an experience would also point out the requirements for the preparation of art work for a poster to be reproduced by either of these two methods.

While letterpress and offset printing would be limited to the commerical printer, the following comparatively simple methods for duplicating a poster can be developed within the realm of the school:

     SILK SCREEN PRINTING

     STENCIL PRINTING

     BLOCK PRINTING

SILK-SCREEN PRINTING

Silk-screen printing is a widely-used stencil technique for reproducing a design. The design may range from one color to a number of colors. It may be reproduced on paper, poster board, wood, metal, plastic, glass, cloth, or on many other kinds of surfaces. The material on which the design is to appear may be in either a two-dimensional or three-dimensional form. Posters, car cards, displays, and illustrations used in advertising are often reproduced by the silk-screen printing process. It is also a very popular medium for applying color and design to toys, games and furniture; labels on bottles, cans, plastic containers, boxes. It would appear that there are infinite possibilities and uses for the silk-screen printing process.

There are numerous occasions in the school program when a poster is needed in quantity, from one-half dozen to fifty or one hundred or more copies. The silk-screen printing process is presented here as it relates to the reproduction of school posters.

Basically the silk-screen printing process is the forcing of paint through a piece of stretched silk on which a design has been applied. The design is formed on the silk by

blocking out some of the mesh and leaving the part to be printed open. The illustration shows a screen prepared to print the letter "T". The area around the "T" has been blocked out and the silk forming the "T", left open. The following steps are required to reproduce the "T" the number of times desired:

1. SCREEN PLACED OVER PAPER ON WHICH "T" IS TO BE PRINTED.

2. SILK-SCREEN PAINT POURED AT ONE END.

3. PAINT PULLED OVER THE SCREEN BY MEANS OF A SQUEEGEE.

4. SCREEN LIFTED SHOWING "T" PRINTED ON PAPER.

The same "T" may be reproduced in reverse by blocking out the "T" on the silk and leaving the area around it open. With this approach, the background would be printed and the "T", itself, would assume the color of the paper on which it is being printed. Although there are many kinds of materials and numerous techniques involved in silk-screen printing, including photography, the example shown here is fundamentally the silk-screen printing process.

EQUIPMENT, TOOLS AND MATERIALS

The following equipment is necessary for silk-screen printing:

1. BASEBOARD. The baseboard may be either a piece of heavy plywood or an old drawing board. It should be larger on all sides than the printing frame, which is to be mounted on it.

2. PRINTING FRAME. A printing frame is a simple, wooden frame on which the silk is stretched and stapled. It should be larger than the design which is to be printed. To be safe, allow 2 to 3 inches extra space all the way around the frame.

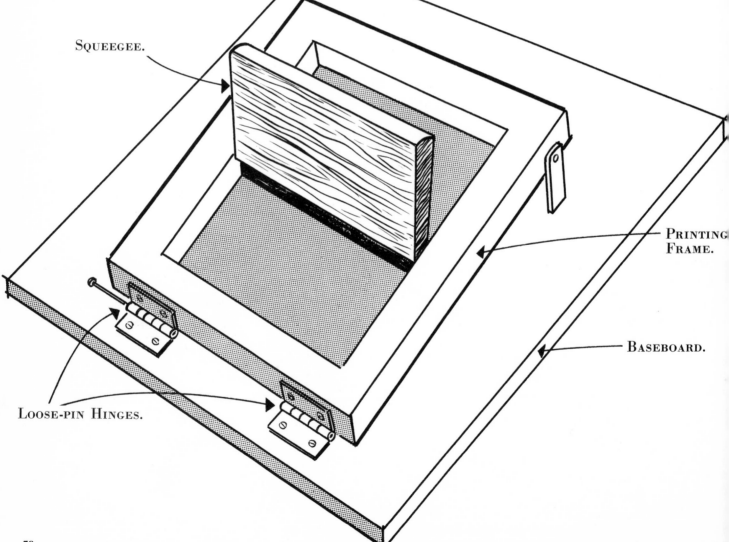

SQUEEGEE.

PRINTING FRAME.

BASEBOARD.

LOOSE-PIN HINGES.

3. LOOSE-PIN HINGES. Loose-pin hinges are used to attach the printing frame to the baseboard. This type of hinge is suggested because it allows easy removal of the printing frame from the baseboard. This is important, particularly when the design is more than one color, therefore requiring two or more printing frames.

4. SQUEEGEE. The squeegee, made of rubber, is used to pull the paint across the screen. Its size is determined by the size of the screen. The squeegee should be large enough so that the paint can be pulled across the surface of the silk in one stroke.

5. SILK. While other fabrics, such as organdy, may be used, silk is recommended because of its durability and better quality of workmanship. A medium-fine mesh silk will serve the purpose for most school needs. The silk must be stretched drum-tight on the frame. This may be accomplished by pulling it tight as it is being stapled to the side of the frame.

Tools that should be available for silk-screen printing would include: scissors, cutting knives, brushes, stapler, steel straight-edge.

The following materials are necessary for silk-screen printing:

1. Silk-screen paint, assorted colors. Silk-screen paint may be either oil or water base.

2. Adhering fluid. This is used in transferring a design made with stencil film to the silk screen.

3. Removing fluid. Removing fluid is used to remove stencil film from the silk.

4. Stencil film. This is a film of colored lacquer laminated to a sheet of glassine paper.

5. Transparent base. Transparent base is added to silk-screen paint to improve the working quality of the paint. It also gives a transparent quality to the paint and is used when there is over-printing in the design.

6. Extender base. Extender base is used to cut the cost of printing. It may be added to paint to extend the colors without reducing their strength.

7. Glue.

8. Tusche.

9. Water tape and masking tape.

10. Stencil filler.

11. Reducers. Kerosene or varnalene may be used to reduce the consistency of oil base silk-screen paint. They may also be used in the cleaning of the screen.

SILK-SCREEN STENCILS

Basic to successful silk-screen printing is the preparation of the screen. There are several methods by which this may be done.

1. THE BLOCK-OUT METHOD

   A. Place the design to be printed beneath the silk screen.

   B. Trace the design to be printed on the silk.

   C. Block out the silk screen around the design with stencil filler. When the stencil filler dries, the screen is ready for printing.

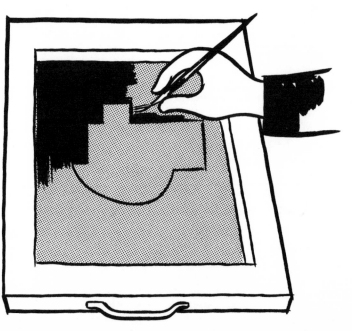

2. **Paper Stencils.** This method is used for short runs and may be described as follows:

A. Cut design out of paper.

B. Place a sheet of waste paper on the base-board beneath the screen.

C. With the screen raised, lay the paper stencil in position.

D. Lower the screen and pour silk-screen paint on one end.

E. Squeegee the paint over the screen and the paper design beneath it will adhere to it.

F. With the paper stencil now adhered to the screen, it is ready for printing.

3. THE TUSCHE METHOD. With this technique the design is actually painted on the screen with liquid tusche, which provides the designer the opportunity to stipple, spatter or dry-brush to get unusual effects.

    A. Place design to be printed beneath screen.

    B. Transfer design to screen, using Tusche.

    C. After design is complete, coat the entire screen with a mixture of water and glue (approximately $\frac{1}{2}$ and $\frac{1}{2}$).

    D. When glue is dry, wash the screen on both sides with kerosene. Those areas where Tusche has been applied will wash off, leaving the desired design.

    E. Place screen on a piece of newspaper and wash further to remove all particles of Tusche. The screen should then be ready for printing.

4. STENCIL FILM. This is a film of colored lacquer laminated to a sheet of glassine paper so that it can be cut and peeled off. The film must be cut without cutting the glassine backing. When using the stencil film technique, it must be remembered that the part that is peeled away is the part that will be printed eventually.

   A. Tape a piece of stencil film over the design.

   B. With a stencil knife, cut around the design and peel off areas to be printed. (If the design is printed in one color, cut the entire design on one piece of stencil film. If it is more than one color, a separate piece of film will have to be used for each color.)

   C. Place completed film stencil under the silk screen frame.

   D. With a small rag, apply adhering fluid to a portion of the screen. Rub over this briskly with a dry rag. Continue until entire screen is covered and film is adhered. Do not over-soak the screen with adhering fluid or the film will dissolve.

   E. Stand screen on edge to dry. After it has dried, peel off the glassine backing sheet.

   F. Fill in the open part of the screen with paper tape. Use stencil filler to touch up spots on the design. The screen is ready for printing now.

GUIDE TECHNIQUES

Once the prepared screen is hinged in place on the base-board it will always come down on the same spot. However, it is important that the paper or poster board, on which the design is being printed, is positioned properly beneath the screen each time. This is even more critical when silk screening a design having two or more colors. There are two methods suggested here for assuring accurate registration:

1. When printing on poster board, squares of the same thickness as the poster board may be used as guides.

2. Tagboard or heavy paper, cut and folded, also serve well as registry guides.

Sequence of steps required in the printing
of a poster in four colors.

CARE OF THE SILK SCREEN

If there is to be a re-run of a design, the screen may be stored with the design on it. Be sure that the printing inks have been thoroughly removed from the screen before storing.

On the other hand, a design may be removed from the silk and the same screen used again with another design. The method for cleaning the silk would depend on the method used in applying the design in the first place. For example, when stencil film is used on the silk a special removing fluid must be used to wash the design off of the silk. Lacquer-base stencil filler may be cleaned from the silk with removing fluid. Warm water and soap will wash water-base glue from the silk.

With proper care and thorough cleaning, the silk may be used over and over many times.

STENCIL PRINTING

The stencil technique may be used in the designing of a single poster as well as in making duplicates of a poster. It is basically the blocking out of some areas of a design while applying a specific color to another area. In stencil painting or printing the paints are applied by an airbrush, a hand air gun or stencil brush. With this technique it is possible to get graded tonal qualities in the design. Spattering and stippling are also characteristic of stencil printing.

In reproducing a poster design the stencil printing technique is recommended when there are a small number of duplicates to be made.

A. Prepare the master poster design in color, actual size, following the suggestions discussed in preceding chapters of this book. A poster to be reproduced by this method should be kept relatively simple.

B. Cut a stencil for each color. For example, a background shape or an illustration may represent one color in a two-color poster and would require one stencil. The lettering may represent another color, calling for an additional stencil. The stencil may be made by tracing that part of the design represented by one color on to a piece of heavy paper and cutting it out with a sharp knife. Acetate may also be used for stencils. Lay the acetate over the master poster design and cut away that which would form one color. Repeat this for the second color and again for each additional color.

C. Using rubber cement, fix the first stencil to a piece of poster board.

D. The color for this stencil may then be applied with an airbrush, a hand spray gun, or a stencil brush.

E. After the paint is dry remove this stencil and proceed with the stencil for the second color.

When making several duplicates of a poster by the stencil method, print all of one color first. Then go back and repeat this step for each stencil.

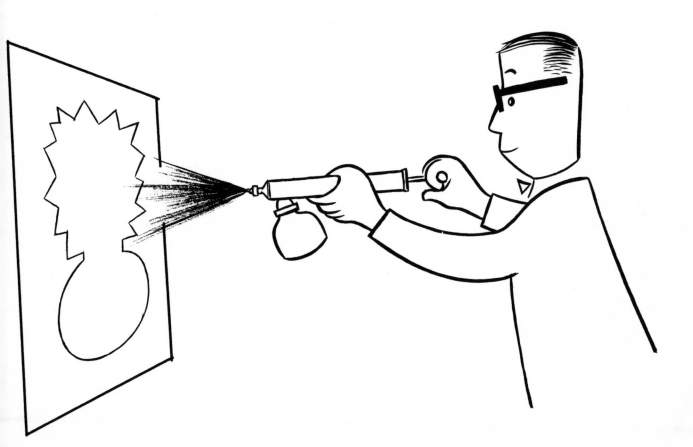

BLOCK PRINTING

Wooden blocks as well as rubber blocks are often used commercially to reproduce posters and car cards. These materials as well as linoleum may be used in duplicating school posters. For short runs a design may be cut from heavy cardboard and mounted on wood. In each case, a separate block must be prepared for each color in the design.

Posters to be reproduced by this method should be designed with areas of flat colors and bold lines in lieu of fine shading and delicate lines.

One marked difference between this printing method and the two others described in this chapter is that the blocks are prepared in reverse. In silk screen printing and stencil printing the color is applied *through* the screen or stencil. In block printing the color is applied *from* the raised surfaces of the block.

    A. Prepare the master design for the poster in color, actual size.

    B. Make tracings for each color.

    C. Reverse these tracings and transfer them to the block (wood, rubber, linoleum, cardboard).

    D. Cut the block.

    E. Print the poster, one color at a time.

Block printing is done with a variety of types of equipment from the relatively simple hand press to the somewhat complex letterpress, used by commercial printers. Basically it is a matter of inking the prepared block, placing it in position against the poster board, applying pressure, and removing it. In schools where there is no special printing equipment:

    A. Spread newspapers on the floor.

    B. Place poster board on newspapers.

    C. Ink the block with a brayer.

    D. Place block on poster board.

    E. Apply pressure by standing on block.

    F. Remove block.

In duplicating a poster by the block printing method, it is also more efficient to print all of one color at a time.

ADDITIONAL SUGGESTIONS

The methods for reproducing school posters decribed here have considerable versatility and lend themselves to experimentation. While it is important to know each process and the basic steps involved, there are many opportunities for unusual effects that should not be overlooked. Some suggestions along this line are:

A. In the process of printing a poster, change the color combinations. Even though the same basic design may be used throughout a single "run", changes in color combinations will give added variety.

B. Try using two different colors at the same time on the same silk screen. Note the unusual and ever-changing blending effects.

C. Experiment with using contrasting colors at the same time on a single block.

D. Combine the different processes. For example, a background effect may be sprayed through a stencil and the illustration block printed on top of this.

E. Combine hand lettering with one of the processes.

F. Use shapes of colored paper in combination with one of the processes.

Each of the printing processes described here becomes more fascinating with a creative approach.

In Memoriam: Martin Luther King Jr., a poster by Romare Bearden. Courtesy, List Art Posters, Boston and New York City.

*The American Dream by Art Bevacqua. Courtesy,
the Museum of Modern Art, New York. Gift of
Joseph H. Heil.*

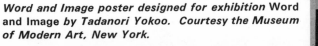

Word and Image poster designed for exhibition Word
and Image *by Tadanori Yokoo. Courtesy the Museum
of Modern Art, New York.*

BRIDGET RILEY March 2-27, 1965 Richard Feigen Gallery New York

Poster by Bridget Riley. Courtesy, Poster Originals, Limited, New York.

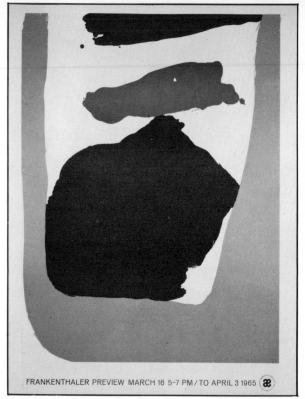

FRANKENTHALER PREVIEW MARCH 16 5-7 PM / TO APRIL 3 1965

Poster by Helen Frankenthaler. Courtesy, Poster Originals, Limited, New York.

Poster by Ben Shahn. Courtesy, the Museum of Modern Art, New York. Gift of the CIO Political Action Committee.

for full employment after the war
REGISTER VOTE
CIO POLITICAL ACTION COMMITTEE

NEW YORK

IS EATING

IT UP!

LEVY'S

REAL JEWISH RYE

Poster by Robert Gage, 1952. Courtesy, the Museum of Modern Art, New York. Gift of Doyle Dane Bernbach, Inc.

AMERICAN AIRLINES
707
JET FLAGSHIP

SAN FRANCISCO

Olympia

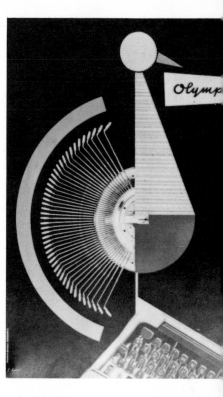

Olympia

BOGOTA
Colombia

BRANIFF International AIRWAYS

THE PLAY OF THE WEEK

A NEW EXPERIENCE IN HOME ENTERTAINMENT
BROADWAY THEATRE IN YOUR LIVING ROOM ★
TWO-HOUR TELEDRAMAS FEATURING TOWERING
PERFORMERS. HELEN HAYES, JUDITH ANDERSON,
HUME CRONYN, DANE CLARK, ELI WALLACH, NINA
FOCH, OTHERS ★ SHOWCASING THE BRILLIANT
WORKS OF LITERARY GIANTS. ANTON CHEKHOV,
JOHN STEINBECK, GEORGE BERNARD SHAW, SEAN
O'CASEY, GRAHAM GREENE, JEAN-PAUL SARTRE,
AUGUST STRINDBERG, OTHERS ★ THE FINEST
SERIES IN THE FIELD OF TV ENTERTAINMENT.
WATCH WBAL-TV 11 FOR TIMES AND DATES
OF ★ THE PLAY OF THE WEEK, EVERY WEEK.

WBAL TELEVISION 11

For a Head Start on Success-Choose an Olympia

Olympia
Precision Typewriters

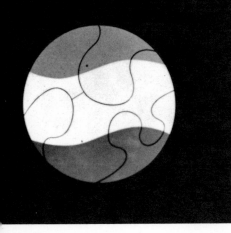

s. An exhibition of braintwisters sponsored by
Cola Company for the exasperation of the public,
y through Friday 9 am-6 pm February 8, to March 21,
Pepsi-Cola Exhibition Gallery, 500 Park Avenue.

*Poster by Peter Gee courtesy Henri Ghent, Assistant
Director, Brooklyn Institute of Arts and Sciences,
Brooklyn, New York.*

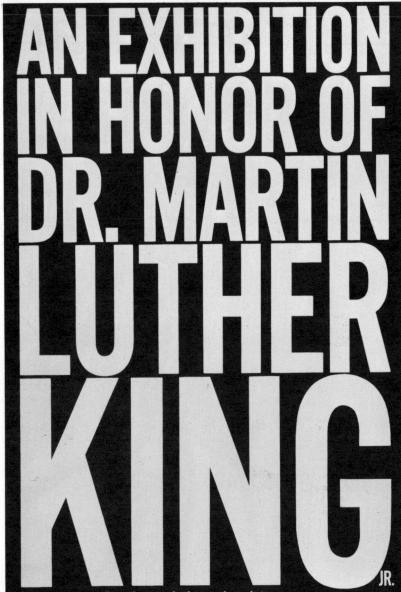

AN EXHIBITION
IN HONOR OF
DR. MARTIN
LUTHER
KING JR.

Contemporary American painting and sculpture
donated by artists to be sold for the benefit of
Southern Christian Leadership Foundation

On view October 31 through November 3
at The Museum of Modern Art
11am to 10pm, Sunday 12 noon to 6pm
Admission free, entrance at 4 West 54 Street

Richard Anuszkiewicz, Romare Bearden, Peter Bradley, Alexander Calder, Sam Gilliam,
Bob Gordon, Adolph Gottlieb, Al Held, Charles Hinman, Richard Hunt, Jasper Johns,
Daniel Johnson, Don Judd, Ellsworth Kelly, Lee Krasner, Jacob Lawrence, Al Leslie,
Jack Levine, Norman Lewis, Alexander Liberman, Roy Lichtenstein, Richard Lippold,
Jacques Lipchitz, Tom Lloyd, William Majors, Marisol, Robert Morris, Robert Motherwell,
Louise Nevelson, Barnett Newman, Isamu Noguchi, Kenneth Noland, Claes Oldenburg,
Jules Olitski, Ray Parker, Jackson Pollock, Fairfield Porter, Robert Rauschenberg,
Ad Reinhardt, Mark Rothko, Bettye Saar, Raymond Saunders, George Segal, Tom Sills,
Tony Smith, Theodoros Stamos, Saul Steinberg, Frank Stella, Mark di Suvero,
Bob Thompson, Andy Warhol, Tom Wesselmann, H. C. Westermann, Charles White,
Jack White, Jacky Whitten, list incomplete

Amerikansk Pop-kons
(106 former av kärlek och förtvivla

29/2-12/4 Alla dagar 12-17, onsdagar 12-
Moderna Muse